Bears for all Seasons
Decorating Tips ❦ Identification Aids

by Rosemary and Paul Volpp

FROM BUCK HILL *with love*
DECORATING (AND FUN) GUIDE

with heartfelt thanks to Gary and Mary Ruddell and
all our friends at Hobby House Press, Inc.

Hobby House Press

Published by

Cumberland,
Maryland 21502

Welcome Back to Buck Hill!

*What fun we have had sharing Christmas with you!
How very much we have enjoyed all the kind things you had to say about
A Beary Merry Christmas! You tell us you used the book as a decorating
guide, an identification guide, a catalog to order from AND, what pleases us
most, a source of great pleasure. Thank you!
You have said you wished you had our column, "Decorating With Teddy
Bears," from the Teddy Bear and friends® magazine in a book by each sea-
son. So we have chosen some of the best-liked examples and made many new
ones for your pleasure — and now present Bears for All Seasons.
We ask you always to remember what Mark Twain said. "The ornament of
a house is the friends who frequent it."
Have fun decorating AND enjoy your family and friends!!!*

Rosemary Volpp

Paul Volpp

ABOUT THE COVER

SPRING	*SUMMER*
Crafts Your Thing? - see page 17.	But Don't Go Near the Water - see page 57.
FALL	*WINTER*
Boooo Who?	"The Groundhog Says" - see page 9.

Additional copies available at $19.95 each plus $1.75 postage from
Hobby House Press, Inc.
900 Frederick Street
Cumberland, MD 21502
or from your favorite bookstore or dealer.

Printed in the United States of America
ISBN: 0-87588-348-6

Dedicated to our children
    Rosemary & Ron Garcia, and P.A. & Teri Volpp
    and the grandchildren — Adam, Amanda, & Jess Garcia; Brian, Andy, & Angie
    Volpp — who will perpetuate our traditions
    and to everyone who enjoys life, people and bears!
Let's celebrate being alive!

From the mountains, to the prairies, grab your imagination and hop right in with "Bo" and "Dearheart." Travel to Buck Hill and ENJOY the CHANGING SEASONS!

Bing, Bing, Bing

No, it is not a typographical error. Our rare old Bing bears are helping us to count down the old year!

Included are: "Der Bingle," circa 1911, brown mohair, 21in (53cm); "Zing the Bing," circa 1920, on wheels, 15in (38cm) long; "Bing Beauty," circa 1911, rotating head, 16in (41cm); and "Bumper Bing" (on top), circa 1920, tumbles, 10in (25cm).

Take any group of your favorite bears, add an old clock, hats and horns, and wait for the Happy New Year!

Good Luck Charms for New Years

A trip to the Little Tokyo section of downtown Los Angeles showed us that our Japanese friends celebrate New Years much as we do.

"Dearheart" has a kimono and "Bo" got a "happy coat." Both are circa 1905 Steiff bears. Their tea party is highlighted by exchanging good luck charms.

Puttin' on Their Top Hats

In the rather formal attire nature gave them, pandas seemed perfect for celebrating New Years.

Whether you have a Midnight Buffet, a Rose Parade Brunch or Between Bowl Games Supper, pandas are fine!

Use one or a group on your coffee table, the breakfast bar or the dining room table. If you stick to black and silver accessories, pandas could even create an "elegant" mood.

At the back we used a *Baby Robbie*, 18in (46cm) contemporary bear made in Israel by Toyland, a division of Caesarea; Glenoit, Ind.

The front row — from the left — an early Dean's Rag Book Co. panda, 9in (23cm); an early "feed me" panda, 14in (36cm) and a circa 1940 Knickerbocker, 9in (23cm).

Ready for the Bowl Games

"Edward," a 30in (76cm) circa 1904 Steiff, who is — in truth — the "Clown Prince" on Buck Hill, ready to ENJOY FOOTBALL!!!

He always wears Paul's old (ahem! excuse me!) letterman sweater. He has a helmet that does not fit so he uses it to hold his Wheat Thins. He has some other favorite things: Sesame Crackers, Red Onion Dip and Cream Soda.

This makes such a great snack table centerpiece, your guests will smile even if their team is losing! Come on — let your bear have a ball on New Year's Day!

Good Luck for the New Year

Did you know it is traditional in some parts of the country to have cabbage and black-eyed peas on New Year's Day to insure good fortune?

Our "cabbage" is soft sculptured cloth. We added construction paper eyes to some of our favorite Merrythought bears.

Masquerading as black-eyed peas are our circa 1940, 20in (51cm) bear, "Agatha," with wishbone button in her ear. In front of her is "Elizabeth," a contemporary limited edition, 15in (38cm). From Harrod's department store in London we got "Margaret," 12in (31cm). With the soft sculpture pea is "Baby Prince," another early Merrythought, 9in (23cm).

Whatever your New Year's Day menu, we wish you your happiest year yet!

Happy New Year!

Diane Gard's *Bearushka* fashion model bear is perfect for our New Year's presentation. Like Rose and Morris Michtom, who made the first American bear, we are teetotallers. However, we were lucky enough to be at a convention in San Francisco and met their grandson, Mark. He sold the family business (Ideal Toy Co.) to a conglomerate and started a winery. He was kind enough to bring each convention guest a souvenir bottle of Michtom wine — a real treasure! Mark passed away in August of 1988.

An awesome display — a bear, a cooler and your choice (sparkling apple juice would do as well).

Bearushka is mohair, fully jointed, 20in (51cm).

Michtom Wineries is owned by Mark Michtom. The Grandson of Morris Michtom, who in 1902 invented the American Teddy Bear and founded Ideal Toy Corp.

This bottle is a souvenir of the Great Western Teddy Bear Show & Gathering, July 4-7, 1985.

The Cherry Tree Tea

"Bo" and "Dearheart," 24in (61cm) circa 1905 Steiffs celebrate Washington's birthday with cherry tarts and honey tea.

Their hatchet candy containers, filled with red hots, are circa 1930. The hatchets give a good excuse to explore Washington stories with grandchildren or your grade school students.

Sweet Valentines!

We combined two gifts — a heart-shaped grapevine basket from our daughter and a pink 8in (20cm) *Rosie* bear given to us by an adopted bear family son and came up with a PERFECT valentine! The shredded colored paper is a newer item, available at most card shops.

You might want to add one of Hermann's Special valentine Bears. The white bear has pink heart flocking on her ruff, is 12in (30cm), made of wool and cotton and has **pink** paw pads. The smaller red bear (limited to 500) is 8½in (22cm).

A grand Valentine threesome!

Rosie is by contemporary artist Paula Egbert.

The Groundhog Sez

The Weatherlady groundhog (Equal Employment Opportunity, remember?) says, "Don't worry about these silly shadows! The sunshine is in your heart!!" Listening intently are bears by Suzan and Heather De Pee. Daughter, Heather, is only ten years old!

From the Suzy Zoo collection we made a marmot into a groundhog. Our snow is cotton and the log is ceramic.

"Blue Bow Bear," is 15in (38cm) and "Pink Bow Bear," 16in (41cm). Both are made of curly mohair.

Remember Raphael Tuck?

The beautiful old valentines were reproduced recently in basket form. We formed a fan of metallic paper and slipped Linda Spiegel's *Derrick Guy* (from 1985) inside. Basket from card or gift shop. *Derrick Guy*, 10in (25cm).

FEBRUARY

Caught by Cupid

An old Rose O'Neill *Kewpie* post card inspired this setting. Our daughter's circa 1950s *Kewpie*, 27in (69cm), smiles approvingly at the sweethearts "Tiddlywink" and "Bear Horner," both circa 1905 Steiff bears, 20in (51cm) tall. "Bear Horner's" gift is a rose in an old *Kewpie* vase with a teddy on it.

This is simplicity itself. Make a headband and add some kind of gift.

Another Tuck Treatment

A small Raphael Tuck basket holds *Valentina* and *Rosemary* and they are oh, so pleased. The bears are by Barbara King.

Valentina is acrylic, 9½in (24cm). *Rosemary* is German mohair, 17in (43cm).

They are displayed on a tray to move wherever needed.

Love Story, Times Two

The painting was an anniversary gift from Paul — also a perfect valentine.

"If I could sit across
  the porch from God,
I'd thank Him for lending
  me you."
—by our friend Flavia Weeden.

The little bears, *Herman* and *Marion*, 7in (18cm), were made by contemporary artist Barbara Sixby.

If you do not have a favorite painting, the card shop is chuck full of cards with great statements. Combine a card with two small bears. This one is easy to repeat at intervals for banquets.

Grandchildren Are for Loving!

Indeed, they are!

The cup our daughter gave us. Your drug store, market or card shop has delightful ones! The bear is 4½in (12cm) and has a chain with a metal "L Dream" tag on his neck and a cloth tag on his side, "Made for Charm Co."

Add some flowers and you have a valentine.

This is another one that would be easy to repeat at low cost for a banquet-type requirement.

FEBRUARY

When Irish Eyes are Smiling

"O'Bo McVolpp" at least hums along as "Dearheart O'Shaunassey" accompanies him on the harp. "Bo" and "Dearheart" are 24in (61cm) circa 1905 Steiffs.

We used some finery from the Party Shop; my mother made the vest and shawl.

Dress your bears up to put them in the spirit for St. Patrick's Day.

Faith and Begora!

Paddy with his pig is always appropriate for St. Patrick's Day! Our contemporary "Paddy" is by Dean's Rag Book Co. of England. We gave him a green ribbon collar and a hat. He is 13in (33cm) tall. His friend, "Ol' Ms," the pig, is circa 1915, completely jointed and 9in (23cm) tall. This set up is easy to repeat at intervals for a luncheon or banquet. *Erin Go Braugh!*

MARCH

The Little Brown Bear —

lived in a hole in a hollow tree, in a bed of leaves, according to the delightful story by Johnny Gruelle.

When the grass turns green again, he jumps out of bed — ready for spring!

We had a lot of fun bringing this story to life with the House of Nisbet's Celebrity Collection reproduction of the *Little Brown Bear* — one of our favorites.

Watch for logs while picnicking in the mountains — they make <u>wonderful</u> bear holders!

Little Brown Bear is 13in (30cm).

A Wagon Full of Paddies

If you cannot choose just one Irish bear, fill a wagon full and have that much more fun on St. Patrick's Day!

Our wagon, circa 1910, is an original of one that is being beautifully reproduced.

Pulling the wagon is *Paddy, the Irish Bear*, a limited edition by Nisbet. He is 15in (38cm) and made of alpaca and mohair, circa 1970.

Sharing a ride are left to right: *Murphy* by Lori Gardiner, 16in (41cm); *Ol Paddy* by Bev Miller, 12in (31cm); and *Darby* by Loretta Botta, 17in (43cm). These are all contemporary artist bears.

The luck of the Irish to you all!

One Potato, Two Potatoes

Contemporary bear artist Sue Kruse's *leprechaun* looks for a pot of gold resting on what else — a bag of Irish potatoes! The little fellow is 7in (18cm), made of acrylic and carries his own shillelagh!

Two of Elaine Fujita Gamble's wee folk play at the bottom. Both are 4in (10cm).

Easy to repeat on a banquet table — one small bear to one or two potatoes.

The Joys of Spring Tra La!

From a lovely reader whose ears tell her what delightful things there are to see came the suggestion for this jump rope centerpiece.

She sent this little jingle. Maybe some of you sang it growing up:

Teddy Bear, Teddy Bear turn around
Teddy Bear, Teddy Bear touch the ground
Teddy Bear, Teddy Bear show your shoes
Teddy Bear, Teddy Bear read the news
Teddy Bear, Teddy Bear be excused!

Our circa 1906 Steiff "Teddy Terrific" came with his sailor suit and jump rope — so he was perfect! He is 9in (23cm).

Spring brought not only the crocus and daffodils, but jumping rope, remember?

Thank you, Mrs. Derks!

When Does a Party Start?

Before you open the door! Sometimes decorations move OUTSIDE! To greet our guests for Easter brunch, at the rear, in a 1913 Gendron pedal car, are "Edward," circa 1903, 30in (76cm) and *Billy Possum*, circa 1909. On the hood is "Mouse," circa 1907, 7in (18cm).

Riding in Bartholomew's Bearcat in front are "Bo," circa 1905, 24in (60cm) and by his side, the small size 8in (20cm), *Jackie Jubilee* bear. All are made by Steiff. Add baskets and flowerpots to please you!

Baskets & Bunnies & Birds & Bears

One of our favorite decorations is a small basket with bluebirds hot glued to the handle. The bunnies are made from infants' anklets. The bear is by contemporary artist Regina Brock and is 6in (15cm) tall. Combinations are unlimited!

APRIL

There is Still Hope

At this wonderful season of the year when all things come to life again, we present 20in (51cm) "Still Hope," a circa 1907 bear by the Aetna Bear Co. of America.

"Still Hope" was named after an early ancestor who was scalped by the Indians and left for dead. She recovered, however, and lived to be 110! If things are not going your way, just remember, there is "Still Hope!"

We love the way he peers around his big jar of candy! Jelly beans, anyone?

Easter Express

Using bears made by artists and our set of 1956 Lionel Girl's Trains with some fake grass and Easter eggs was all we needed for this decoration. Left to right: Bev Miller's *Bunny Bear*, 10in (25cm), Karine Masterson's *Butterfly Bear*, 11½in (29cm), and Eileen Markarian's *Dusty Dreams*, 9in (23cm).

Crafts Your Thing?

Then this is one for you! My mom made the basket from a pattern. Donna Hodges' bear, *Michelle*, is attired in a hand-crocheted dress and bonnet. We love the combined effect!

Get out the sewing machine and crochet hook! Spring is coming!

Michelle is mohair, 8½in (22cm).

APRIL

Walking Down a Country Lane

For a window ledge! All our flower shops have variations of this country fence. Prop it against your kitchen window and steady it with a bear. Isn't it fun? The Easter hat (with ears) comes off and you have a regular bear.

Lil Bear Blue by Joan Davis, 5½in (14cm).

Bears-a-Poppin

All new favorites! Gloria Rosenbaum's *Rosenhare* proudly shows off his own Easter basket. Aren't the reproduction 1930 tipped fur bears from Merrythought great? Choose tissue to match your room.

Rosenbare is 17in (43cm).

Merrythought bears are 7in (18cm).

APRIL

The Egg Factory

With six grandchildren, we need lots of Easter eggs so we put "Bo" and "Dearheart," both circa 1905, 24in (61cm) Steiffs, in charge.

"Bo" handles the orders and "Dearheart" consults a book for design ideas.

At the left, a contemporary Hermann 11in (28cm) made for the 1986 Ontario ILTBC Convention is very busy painting green eggs.

Two circa 1950, 8in (20cm) open-mouth Steiff teddies are in charge of a cart filled with eggs.

The final inspector, *Rosemary*, 3in (8cm), riding in the cart, is by contemporary artist Dickie Harrison.

Let your bears color eggs — it is a winning combination!

Muffins Anyone?

The next time muffins are on your menu — let a bear be in charge of the serving basket. Our *Muffin Man* by Nancy Crowe was absolutely perfect! Any bear who would not eat the muffins will do.

Muffin Man, of wavy mohair is 14in (35cm).

Fancy That!

"Luana," a very early Steiff with blank button, 13in (33cm) — and named for Miss Hawaii International, holds our circa 1910 papier-mâché egg that is decorated with Roosevelt type bears.

"Luana's" Easter hat is by Hawaiian designer Eric Eugene Chandler.

A bear, an egg and a fancy hat — that is all it takes — fancy that!

Roy's Funny Bunny

Roy Howey's *Funny Bunny*, 15in (38cm), presents Paul's toys from the late 1920s, a blanket bunny, cloth rabbit and a wooden pull toy rabbit. New and old. Accent with yellow tissue and daffodils.

"Lyda Rose Quackenbush"

— ready for a ride into the country in her Goose Caboose (by Pruitt's Place). "Lyda Rose" is presumed to be English, circa 1930.

With her roses and pink streamers, she reinforces the English country garden feeling.

On a Lamp Table

— by an easy chair, we find *Rosemary, the Intrepid Collector*, circa 1985 by Lori Gardiner, 19in (48cm), acrylic. She has a new English rose and Netts doll-rabbit-bear keeps her company. Netts bear is mohair, 15in (38cm). Lynn West's colorful *Jester Bear* is 24in (61cm). He stands in front of a Lynn West basket with a beautiful Charlene Kinser rabbit in it.

At the left — watching the picture being taken — are a very early Steiff lamb and bear.

APRIL

Mantle Magic

Roses that seem to be vining over a fence give a quiet beauty to the Easter mantle. We dearly love our painting of the rabbit and butterfly by Forbes. Completing the feeling of peace and purity are the white F.A.O. Schwarz Steiff (special for Christmas, 1988) and, on the right, the Steiff *Muzzle Bear*.

In-a-Box

— of shredded metallic paper is the 1988 limited edition Steiff *Teddy Baby* made for Peter Wolf of Germany, 12in (30cm). All shades of pink and oh, so pleasing!

Going Upstairs — Easter

We have used a "constant," a particular location over and over to show how one spot changes with the seasons. The Christmas garland is replaced with one of spring flowers and ribbons. Anna Lee rabbits, circa 1978, add whimsy.

Waste Basket Turned Vase

Good anywhere! We found a Gordon Frasher teddy bear wastebasket that was much too pretty for waste. We filled the bottom with crumpled paper and put artificial forsythia and lilies in a bouquet on top. Accompanied by a small woven basket and some ceramic ducks, it was perfect for the sink top of our downstairs bath.

APRIL

Out the Kitchen Window

You spend so much time in the kitchen, make it a fun place to be. Bright flowers in vases of unusual sizes, bears and rabbits and any of God's creatures, mix and match to your heart's content! We have some Anna Lee aviator ducks coming in for a landing!

The Coffee Pot

— does not have to be drab! We put a clear glass candy container filled with multi-colored Easter eggs next to it and topped it off with a brown sitting bear with a "Danker" label, circa 1950, 7in (18cm). "Brown Brew" is his name and he sits on the sink when the coffee pot is in use. His friend is an Anna Lee rabbit.

Of Lights and Flowers
— new from Carol Black is the blossom-trimmed rabbit basket complete with bunny, duck and hand-painted eggs. Dressed in pink organdy, *Carol* bear puts the finishing touches to this delight. The bear is mohair, 15in (38cm) and musical. What fun to have Easter lights, too!

Television Top Rating —
goes to "Serenity," circa 1905 Steiff, 24in (61cm). She has an Easter hat made by a lady who was a real milliner. She also has a lace collar, my beads and her own small basket. "Serenity" was one of our first old bears and is still at the top!

At the Top of the Stairs

— with the "Peaceable Kingdom" painting — on the verse stand is Loretta Botta's yellow bear with green eyes and pads and dressed in flower petals, circa 1985, 14in (35cm). Most unusual. In the artificial shrubs to the left are bears by Dot Kunkle and Barbara Burbeck. In the log are Bev Miller's *Putting on the Bunny* bear, 10in (25cm), and her *Bear and Rabbit*. Standing in front of the big limited edition (20 only) Hermann we call "Nutmeg" are Lori Gardiner's *Wendy Bear* (with antique toy watch) and a *Bee in Her Bonnet* mechanical bear. Both are acrylic and 16in (40cm). Pick a color and group bears of the same shade for a pleasing effect.

A Robins Nest —
is a sure sign of spring. We added one to our ceramic log vase filled with yellow spring flowers. The bear cubs by Robyn of Idyllyld frolic underneath.

Visitors Love It!
We have bears in the wallpaper in the guest bath. From Standard Brands Paint Stores.

Not Another —
Teddy Bears Picnic! Oh, yes! This one is on top of the bed in a guest room. We had these Russ Berrie bears before we really started collecting! There can be countless variations.

APRIL

Tissue, Anyone?

So many in our family have allergies, we have Kleenex in every room in the house! A set-up like this takes the "choo" out of "ahchoo!" *Bruinsnout* by Ballard Baines (ours is the prototype!), 16in (41cm), always makes me smile. That is what a bear should do!

Rembrandt Rabbit

An old "see through" Easter egg I made some 20 years ago is being touched up by Anna Lee's new bear. He loves to paint! Most grandchildren and bears do, too!

APRIL

"Amazing Grace"

Our early mechanical Bing bear, circa 1912, (her head moves from side to side), complete with button under her arm, has an antique chicken candy container filled with a lilac to match her lavender bow. Accent with a purple butterfly!

"Amazing Grace" is 12in (30cm).

The Rabbit Family Basket

— from Teddy's Tracks in Plymouth, Michigan, came this extra special treat! Mr. & Mrs. Rabbit and baby are a part of the basket! Look for one!

The small mohair rabbit and bear in the basket came from ABC's "Over the Rainbow" convention. See their wings; they can fly!

Both by Wendy Lockwood — both 6½in (16cm).

APRIL

And Spring Shall Come

"Grand Fellow," a 28in (71cm) circa 1905 Steiff, reads his favorite book to contemporary artist Kaylee Nilan's "Baby Holey Moley" and *Baby Beaver*. Both babies are approximately 10½in (27cm) tall.

Our Bob Raikes original owl listens, too. The owl is 11in (28cm) tall.

Have fun combining lots of animals. Spring would bring all the new babies out to enjoy the flowers!

And Spring Shall Come is by Dean Walley.

This is so simple; it is almost reverent and makes a wonderful Easter brunch centerpiece.

Fun with Off Colors

Not always associated with the pastels of Easter — try an unusual blue reproduction of an antique chicken candy dish.

Guarding the dish is a charming fellow of antique white terry cloth (with bright green eyes) by Cathy Orlando. The bear is 7½in (19cm).

Floating on Clouds

When the first girl grandchild was born into our family (Amanda Rosemary), her Uncle Paul made her this heavenly highchair. Abandoned highchairs make royal thrones for bears. Watch for one at garage sales — then go wild painting it!

Sitting in the chair is Barbara Burbeck's "Pink Divinity," acrylic, 18in (45cm), holding a sock rabbit.

On the moon is Bev Miller's *Rabbit in Bear Suit*. On the cloud is Bev's bear who thinks he is a rabbit. Both are acrylic, 11in (28cm).

Surprised?

You bet! When the eggs this rabbit was delivering hatched — out popped bear cubs! (We should be so lucky!)

The rabbit, by Suzanne Marx, is no longer being produced.

The bears with red bows are a limited edition (500 only) by Merrythought, mohair, 5in (11cm). In the blue tulip dish is a Regina Brock mohair bear, 6in (15cm).

This sets up nicely on a tray.

Rollin' Down the Bunny Trail!

It can happen! Probably tired from delivering so many eggs, *Sally* rabbit lassoed Beth Hogan's Bear on Wheels for a ride.

A small bear — a small rabbit — good for a big chuckle!

Set up on a bread plate.

Rabbit by Jane Carlson, felt, 5in (13cm).

Bear on Wheels by Beth Hogan, 3in (8cm).

True Beauty is Simplicity

Here we offer a duck parade. Hold your breath — each duckling has a Steiff button in one webbed foot!

Find new counterparts. Great repeated down a banquet table. We used soft sculpture place mats for the "country road."

Ducks, Steiff, circa 1914 — momma, 5in (13cm); baby, 3in (8cm).

Something Special?

Oh, yes! Only a _very_ special bear could hold this _very_ special basket! Our daughter-in-law decorated it. The egg opened to reveal a note that announced their first child was on the way!

Donna Claustre's _Precious_ is just right! We love these soft stuffed bears who will sit, lounge and cross their legs; they are almost human.

This basket is a family tradition! That baby was 14 years old in November.

Precious is acrylic, 15in (38cm).

APRIL

Our Cabbage Patch Rabbit

A great favorite among visitors, an automata rabbit that pops in and out of the cabbage as a music box plays. Turn of the century, probably French. We found it at Linda Mullins' show!

Also a favorite (whom we call "Myrna Loy" because of her cute nose) is 15in (38cm); possibly Ideal, circa 1920.

Afternoon Tea at the Ritz

Abiner Smoothie has a lady love. Her name is "Marshmallow" and they are enjoying High Tea! The centerpiece rabbit, 31in (79cm) is an old store display piece. Watch for these! It is a mechanical. The hand goes in and out of the purse. "Marshmallow" by Barbara Burbeck is of German acrylic, 19in (48cm).

Gund's *Abiner Smoothie*, seated, 19in (48cm). Bear in book, Bev Miller's *Attic Teddy*, 6in (15cm).

Small Bears a Problem?

No problem! Let a favorite bunny hold a box full. We got our Kamar bunny for our first grandson who is now 16. All six grandchildren had a turn with it.

The small bears are: ballet by Pat Carriker, 2½in (6cm); other two by Dickie Harrison, 3in (8cm).

Tiptoe Through the Tulips

With a tulip for a spring bonnet, this delightful bear (we named her "Tippy Toes") is by Washington State's grand Dutch bear artist, John Port.

I can see a banquet table with nests of tulip bears all down the center and I like it! Some bears might even prefer daffodil chapeaus.

From stem to footpads, "Tippy Toes" is 9in (23cm tall.

APRIL

Up a Tree

The tree was made of a manzanita limb by Neil Emory and we have used it many ways. This time we have smaller bears having springtime fun. All bears are Steiff.

The "star" got to climb the tree. He is a circa 1904 blank button. Also having fun (in green cap and scarf) is a limited edition *Shakespeare Bear* from England. Margaret Strong bears wear the overalls and dress, and the smallest gets to be swung.

All bears are mohair and fully jointed.

Star, 10in (26cm); *Shakespeare*, 7in (18cm); Margaret Strong, 9in (23cm) and *Swing Bear*, 5in (13cm).

How About Harvey?

Speaking of rabbits — do you remember the Jimmy Stewart movie "Harvey" — about an imaginary rabbit? We feel very fortunate to own one of the 12 sets (picture, bear and rabbit) by superb artist Garret Sakamoto (retired) in the early 1980s. Stewart gave his blessing to the project because the profit went to the Los Angeles Zoo. James and Gloria Stewart are great patrons of the zoo.

Bear, mohair, jointed, 11in (28cm).

Rabbit, 5in (13cm).

A Woodland Nursery

If you love the forest like we do — you will love this tribute to nature's mothers. We used cedar branches for a picture perfect bassinet for *Rosie* and her new baby — by contemporary artist Paula Egbert of Seattle, Washington.

Both are made of mohair, — *Rosie* is 7½in (19cm) and *Baby* is 4½in (11cm).

This would be easy and inexpensive to repeat in a banquet or club meeting situation.

A Treasured Book — A Treasured Bear

Paul's mother passed away recently. One of her treasures was a small volume, *I Will Lift Up Mine Eyes*. We find comfort in it.

We had a new "old" bear awaiting a name. In memory of Bess, we call her "The Lady Bess." She is an early Steiff, 14in (36cm). We got her from her original owner so she is special!

It helps to dwell on pleasant memories. A treasured book, a treasured bear — a living memory!!!

All By Myself!

Riding his trike "by myself" is a Suzy Zoo *Hugo Bear* given to us by our daughter. He is contemporary, 15in (38cm), available in most stationery stores and bear shops.

His trike is by Helen and Keith Lentner of Frankenmuth, Michigan.

All the expressions of childhood accomplishment can be interpreted with bears — and savored in remembering! This could be fun for a club contest!

So Many Children

What to do? Love them, of course! From coast to coast we have been told this is the year of the miniature bear!

A great display medium is a shoe house! Ours is a delightful creation by Joanne Adams of Park City, Utah.

Old Woman is 9in (23cm); "children" are 3in (8cm).

To make your own shoe house, check your ceramics shop or wholesale florists (Styrofoam Santa's boots). Also check garage sales for real shoes to adapt to bear apartments. *Tip* — take your bears in your purse so you know they will fit. Looks can be deceiving!

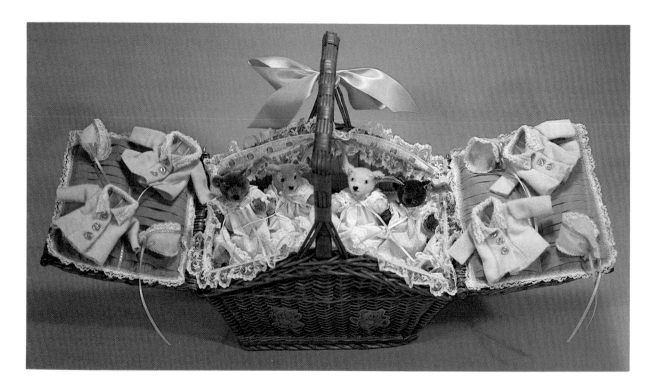

The Quadruplets

This is a perfect Mother's Day centerpiece for those of you who love projects!

Juanita Chidester of Brea, California, started with four, 4in (10cm) contemporary jointed Steiff bears. She made dresses, bonnets and coats. She lined a Knott's Berry Farm jam basket with pink flannel and lace. Doesn't it make a pretty picture? Know what? Juanita is my mother!

A Mother's Memories

When I saw this rocking bear, I was transported in thought to a time when our son was three years old. He rode on his "speedy bike" as we walked his big sister to kindergarten.

Recall a favorite memory and turn it into a centerpiece by combining bears and toys.

Our bear and horse are by contemporary teddy bear artist Lori Gardner. It is 15in (38cm) tall and has a music box inside that plays "Memory" from the Broadway musical "Cats."

Bears in the Kitchen?

Of course! What better place to display and enjoy your collection of small bears!

A cup rack and cups make a perfect display piece. Cups on the left hold Dickie Harrison's *T.R.*, and Pat Carriker bears. Down the center (top to bottom) are 4in (10cm) bears by Lara Zano, Saki Romerhaus and Ballard Baines. In the cups on the right are bears by Dickie Harrison and Laurie Sasaki.

Thank Heaven for Little Girls!

From left: Angela Marie is now seven; on the right, Amanda Rosemary is twelve — but Lori Gardiner's bear, *Megan*, says it all — little girls grow bigger (and sweeter) every day. The mohair bear is 12in (30cm).

Making Cookies

A favorite mother and daughter pastime in our family is baking cookies — then eating them.

We borrowed a doll table and cookware for *"Mrs. Fields"* and little *"Semi Sweet"* to use. The bears are probably Schucos, circa 1950. The larger bear is 11in (28cm) tall; the small bear is 7in (18cm) tall.

By Lamp Light

How many mothers have read how many stories to their children by the flickering light of a kerosene lamp? Our circa 1907 American Aetna bear, "Still Hope," feels quite at home with this lamp. He could have posed for the hand-painted globe!

The lamp was found by a dear friend in a small town in Minnesota. Such a find! Always watch for props like this!

Happy Mother's Day — Yes? — No?

At work at the turn-of-the-century "Excelsior" washing machine is "Momma Rebecca," a 20in (51cm) Yes-No Schuco with soulful eyes. Playing on the floor is "Pretty Baby," a 12in (31cm) Yes-No Schuco. She has an old Steiff elephant whose tag reads, "180ex." "Me Too," an 8in (20cm) Yes-No Schuco, has her own Steiff 75th anniversary elephant. We have come a long way — so have our washing machines.

Company's Coming

— so Donna Claustre's "Rosemary" has dressed baby "Rosebud" in her finery and is about to take the tea things out of the hutch.

All kinds of bears, plus small furniture, would be easy centerpieces for a Mother-Daughter Banquet.

Hutch by Arcade, circa 1930.

"Rosemary," German plush, 10in (26cm).

"Rosebud," 3in (8cm).

Indy 500 — For Collectors of Small Bears

For a less serious note on Memorial Day, try this modern tradition. This became a family project involving grandchildren Amanda, Brian and Andy who contributed cars from the Y.W.C.A. and Cub Scout Pinewood Derbies. Small 4in (10cm) bears became proud drivers. Add a spectators' bench and a checkered flag and the race is on! Great for a Memorial Day pot luck centerpiece.

The "Bearterans"

Our "Bearterans" include "Major Benny Berdoo," a circa 1940 Steiff, 15in (38cm) tall, who does not have a purple heart but one made of red glass. "PVT" is a 20in (51cm) old English bear with a doll's cryer instead of a growler He mans the circa 1920 Marlin cannon. "Bear in Boots" is a 12in (31cm) old Steiff. For navy folks, we have found a souvenir pillow (1919) from the *USS* super-dreadnaught *Arkansas*. If you like, just add some flags and you are all set for Memorial Day celebrating!

MAY

With a Heart That is True

Bridal procession by contemporary teddy bear artist Bev Miller. Large bears are 9in (23cm) tall; small bears are 6in (15cm) tall. What can I say? I am of that generation! I'll be loving you always. Your procession could be just a bride and groom wearing doll outfit or a Snoopy tux under an arch of Styrofoam studded with artificial flowers and ribbons. Great for showers, receptions and anniversaries!

Cutting the Cake

June is *the* month for weddings! "*Bo*" and "*Dearheart*" pose with a cake topped by celluloid dolls from Paul's aunt's wedding in June 1929. "*Dearheart's*" veil was made to match the cake doll's. Old or new cake tops with bears dressed to match are memory-makers for showers and receptions.

How Does Your Garden Grow?

Whether it is beets or bluebells, it is time for spring planting. Our farmer bear by Gerry's Teddy & Crafts of Queensland, Australia, is 17in (43cm) tall.

A bear and a sprinkling can make such an easy spring decoration for banquets and other social functions.

JUNE

Dad's Turn - Breakfast in Bed

It will be great fun, if he does not spill his coffee!

Our "Bruno," a 30in (76cm) circa 1904 Steiff, deserves a treat! He arrived in the United States stuffed around a set of "good" family dishes — used as packing by some former owners!

"Bruno," enjoy!!!

Tending the Garden

— is only one of *Norwood's* tasks. He carries a hammer, file and nails and does carpentry jobs, too. Our "garden" came from a home order catalog. *Norwood*, a troll bear, is the latest creation of Jerry and Morgan Jurdan. Made of West German plush, he is 10in (26cm). Jerry handcrafts his tools.

JUNE

Happy Father's Day!

"Dearheart" got tickets to take "Bo" to the ball game.

You can see, "Bo" "Loves them Angels!" He also brought his mitt to catch fly balls (it was Paul's) <u>AND</u>, his entire collection of baseball cards — one! But can you believe it is the "Buck Hill Aces," 1958? "Dearheart" is <u>not</u> the consummate baseball fan. She brought her Famous Chicken and is working quietly in her chicken coloring book. Such devotion!

Bears are a fun way to display souvenirs you bring home from your favorite sports outing!

You have heard, of course, that baseball cards and bears are among America's "top five" collectibles.

"Bo" and "Dearheart" — 24in (60cm) circa 1905 Steiff.

Congratulations Graduate — the World is Yours

We used a contemporary 18in (46cm) Hermann bear but any bear will do if you dress him in a cap and gown and use a globe as a prop — that is all!

JUNE

Remembering Dad
The Sunday Funnies

Who read *you* the funnies before you accomplished that great feat?

"Poppa Bo," a circa 1905 24in (61cm) Steiff, sits in his turn-of-the-century hand-carved Bavarian chair and reads to "Little Bear Peep," a 20in (51cm) circa 1904 Steiff. She wears an antique lawn hand-embroidered dress and gives complete attention.

"Mistletoe," the only bear we have ever seen with a brown gutta-percha nose, sits on a turn-of-the-century cut-and-sew ball. "Mistletoe" is an 11in (28cm) early Steiff.

Let a family of your bears enjoy the Sunday funnies!

Graduation!

To celebrate and commemorate graduations, we dressed the large-sized Steiff reproduction 1909 bear in a Snoopy graduation outfit. We found pictures of graduations including ours from high school, our daughter's from Mills College and our son's from Stanford, also the grandchildren from preschool and kindergarten. We grouped them together on top of a train case and looped colored ribbon between the photographs. It reminds you — time goes by too quickly!

Goin' Fishing

"P.A. Pooh," 20in (51cm) tall, described by the late Peter Bull as a "nice old English bear," celebrates Father's Day by going fishing. Mr. Bull autographed "Pooh's" foot at a convention in Minnesota. From the fisherman in your family borrow some lures; the pole is from the supermarket. The car is a fun addition but if you do not have one, just let your bear sit on a green napkin or some crumpled green paper (for grass).

A Day at the Train Museum

"Dad," *Humphrey B.* from Australia, is 24in (61cm) from toe to top of his boater hat and has fun showing off his knowledge of old trains to 12in (30cm) *Humphrey, Jr.*

Jr. still has his tag that reads, "Classic Toy Pty. Ltd., Made in Australia 78."

The train is circa 1902, live steam, English and called the Clyde-London North West Railroad.

Did your dad ever take you to climb on the old trains? A great Father's Day outing!

JUNE

On the Right Track

People have asked to see our early Steiff bear named "Ho Hum," 15in (38cm) tall. Here he is having Fourth of July fun with his Freedom Train by Lionel. He and his friend, *Paul*, are working very hard to get their train together properly. *Paul* is by contemporary artists Terry and Doris Michaud and is 12in (31cm) tall. Bears and trains are always a winning combination!

Bang!

Peeking around a big firecracker we made by covering an oatmeal box with red paper and adding a rope "fuse" is our original 1909 Steiff, 20in (51cm). We call him "Lom."

"Lom" came from a delightful little lady who let us have him because she wanted him to be in a "famous" home! She and "Lom" had lived in Newport Beach and Palm Springs so I guess it figures! Her name for him had been "Little Old Man" — hence. "Lom."

This is another set up easy to recreate at small cost for meeting sized numbers.

You Can't Beat It!

"King Arthur," rare circa 1904, 30in (76cm) Steiff (yes, he still has his button) has his turn beating our drum with the Roosevelt bears lithography. Both the bear and the drum are great favorites on Buck Hill.

Remember when you used to make admirals' hats from newspapers? We made one for "King Arthur."

Bears of all sizes with drums (from the toy store or thrift shop) wearing paper hats would be easy to repeat for club, church or family reunion picnics. Simple and fun!

The Lamp Beside the Golden Door

Let us not forget our Statue of Liberty during this season of patriotism!

Our circa 1904 16in (41cm) Steiff bear, whose name is "Irene," was dressed beautifully by California bear artist Vicki Stanard. Did you know "Irene" was the Greek goddess of peace?

You could add a cluster of flags on either side or a bouquet of red, white and blue flowers — or — just drape the bear in gold lamé, cover a cardboard crown and the bear alone helps us all to remember we are "yearning to be free."

Homemade Ice Cream

No self-respecting turn-of-the-century American family would celebrate Independence Day without ice cream "turned by hand." Giving the final crank to his circa 1910 freezer is "Harmles" (with one "s"). New to the Buck Hill gang, he is 24in (61cm) tall, circa 1904, and has a cone nose. The letters on his chest stand for "Kimball Union Academy," a boys' prep school in Meridian, New Hampshire, where "Harmles" was a beloved mascot many years ago. Toy ice cream freezers are difficult to find but worth waiting for. Our bears like "pink" ice cream best.

Ding-A-Ling

So welcome on a hot day in July, the Ice Cream Man! You recognize "Bo," circa 1905 Steiff, 24in (60cm). A good friend found the ice cream cart. Jewels like this do come up at garage sales! Chocolate or strawberry?

Is your group having an ice cream social? Great greeter!

"Another Fine Mess"

Our family enjoys old Laurel and Hardy film festivals at home. A centerpiece of these famous American comedians, 13in (33cm) tall, by contemporary bear artist Bev Miller with a 1930s Buddy L flivver is representative of their many fine films. Add a bowl of buttered popcorn and enjoy the movie! To improvise Laurel and Hardy, choose a fat bear and one much thinner. Both wear bowler hats purchased from a doll shop and one has a little bow tie while the other wears a long tie. You could even pin a little black mustache under Ollie's nose!

But Don't Go Near the Water!

"Teddy Long John," circa 1905 Steiff, 24in (60cm), took his blanket to the beach. He loves to <u>play</u> in the sand, but not <u>sit</u> in it! His <u>pail</u> is circa 1910 with Roosevelt lithography.

By the Sea

Cathy Orlando recreated the delightful Coppertone ad — complete with the little dog.

Perfect table centerpiece for poolside party or backyard barbecue. No sand? Ours is Cream of Wheat. Fooled ya!

Bear, mohair, jointed, 10in (26cm).

Dog, 5½in (14cm).

Aloha Oi!

Whether you have already been, have your tickets to go or are just dreaming about a trip to Hawaii, a great luau decoration is bears dressed in "island finery."

My mom made the shirts for "Bo," circa 1905, 24in (61cm) and "Edward," 1903 Steiff, 30in (76cm). "Edward" is a rare "cone" nose bear. Our 1909 Steiff *Billy Possum*, 12in (31cm), borrowed a grass skirt from Snoopy

Pass the pineapple and poi! Mahalo!

Down to "Craw Dad" Hole

It is August and the livin' is easy! Give your bear a straw hat and a fishing pole and you know where he will go. Perfect for a fish fry or a barbecue. Our bear is by contemporary artists Jerry and Morgan Jurden. He is 14in (35cm) tall and his pole really works!

AUGUST

Sleeping Late

One of the nicest things about summer vacation — no alarm clock to answer to!

"Dearheart," our circa 1905, 24in (61cm) Steiff, luxuriates in her new vine design bed by contemporary artists at the Grand Pa Pa Jingles Bear Company, from the recent Schaumburg, Illinois, convention.

Her dog, 16½in (42cm), circa 1908, awaits her awakening to come outside and play. He has eight buttons with raised STEIFF block letters with the "F" underscored on his collar.

Would your bear like a new bed and nightgown? Do not forget to turn off those alarm clocks.

Pleasant dreams!

AUGUST

Waiting for the School Bus
Meerly A. Bair

Everyone collects something! Guess what *Meerly* collects? SMILES!!! Do you have one for him?

This is one of the most innovative and charming bears to appear in a long time! He <u>always</u> makes us smile! His creator, Gale Cooper, is a lady who loves people. She is a practicing psychiatrist. *Meerly* also has his own book that you can share with grandchildren, or just enjoy yourself.

He wears size 6 loafers and his shirt is a size 2 from Neiman Marcus. He is fully jointed, made of mohair, 24in (61cm). Smile!

Way to Go, Elmo!

Centerpiece for football get-togethers or the Sports Boosters Club! Grandson Adam (at 16) was starting varsity quarterback and also All League. Guess who was proud? Initials "P.V." and "R.V.!"

"Elmo" is *Ezekial* #1 by Maul & Paw Bears, mohair, 24in (60cm).

BELOW:

Awesome! Awesome!

Where you have football, you have cheerleaders! Our favorite this year was "Krissy," the person and the bear! Bear by Bev Miller, 10in (25cm).

RIGHT:

Rah Team!

Perfect to wear to the football game! Just center an artificial mum with a bear, add a ribbon and you are a "Best Dressed" spectator. Our bear is 4in (10cm), circa 1950, from the University of California at Berkley.

Is that Cricket?

No! It is baseball!

"Edward," circa 1903 Steiff, 30in (76cm) wears everybody's sports jacket but he was especially proud of this! Fourteen-year-old grandson, Brian, was part of a Friendship Baseball Team that played in Australia! We made "Edward" share the cap with "Harmles," also a 1903 Steiff, who was actually a sports mascot at a prep school 20 miles from Dartmouth.

The mitt was Paul's in the 1930s. The baseball was signed by Lou Gehrig, the "Iron Man," — baseball player extraordinaire and gentleman!!!

I know what you are thinking. Isn't there <u>anything</u> those Volpps do not collect?

G'Day Mate!

Added to the curriculum at our bear's school this year is an intensive study of the koala and other Australian friends!

In their class in the eucalyptus tree are Charleen Kinser's contemporary koala, 22in (56cm) and a 1950s Steiff koala, 16in (41cm). The blackboard climber is a 5in (13cm) 1950s Steiff koala.

The platypus, maker unknown, is not too attentive.

Isn't it exciting that *Teddy Bear and friends®* now goes into Australia?

Slam — Dunk!

— the boys work so hard at sports! What to do with trophies? When Grandson Andy's team became City Basketball Champ, it was very easy! We arranged the trophy together with that all-time great *Kareem Abdul Jabear!* From North American Bear Co., Inc., *Kareem* is a stretched out 24in (61cm).

Three Strikes, You're Out

Does your family have World Series fever? If so, a perfect companion for watching the games is contemporary artist Bev Miller's *Baseball Shirley*, 9in (23cm) tall. Add a bowl of popcorn, baseball caps, and so forth and pretend you are at the park rooting for the old home team!

The Long and the Short of It

Schuco soccer players, *Bigo Bello*, circa 1950, 11in (28cm) and 3½in (9cm) were used to show off youngest Grandson Jess' trophy! Jess is the youngest, now six — and inspired our own "Anything Bear" (see page 96).

Sports are important to growing up — and so is encouragement!!!

Falling Leaves

Back to nature, the "great decorator," for inspiration! Make a pile of colored leaves or a trail of leaves across a table and add autumn-colored bears for accent. We used "*Orange Blossom*," 11in (28cm); "*Lemon Burst*," 15in (38cm), by contemporary artist Barbara Burbeck; and Bev Wright's "*Butternut*," 11in (28cm). The bears can roll and tumble with the wind. So colorful, simple and lots of fun!

The School Bell Rings!

"Bo" and "Dearheart," both circa 1905, 24in (61cm) Steiff bears are back at their antique school desk, thirsting for knowledge (or mischief?).

Look who the teacher is. It is a circa 1910 Palmer Cox Brownie! These interesting fellows made their debut as drawings on the pages of a children's publication, *St. Nicholas Magazine*, in February 1883. Ours seems to be "homemade" from a pattern (as opposed to manufactured) and is 24in (61cm) tall.

The lesson is from *The Brownie Primer*, circa 1905 — the original price, 35 cents!

It is fun to use another medium with your bears: dolls, *Kewpies*, and so forth.

School desks come in all sizes from about 3in (8cm) up at toy stores.

Good for Back to School nights, PTA meetings or just fun at home!

September Song

Practicing their "do re mis" in the forest school are, in the second row, Merrythought's limited edition 5½in (14cm) trunk bears, hand-signed.

temporary artist Linda Stafford's *Sweet William* made of mohair and fully jointed. Notice his lunch basket full of raspberries. *William* is 6in (15cm) tall.

The wise old owl teacher, 6in (15cm), is a Japanese mechanical; his beak moves and so does his baton. Circa 1950. Watch for goodies like this at garage sales and mall shows.

Bears love music!

SEPTEMBER

Autumn's Song

— the crunch of fallen leaves when you rustle through them.

— the crackle of a bonfire at the marshmallow roast that is your reward for raking the leaves.

Burning leaves and toasting marshmallows are wonderful fall sounds and smells!

Sitting on logs enjoying a marshmallow roast are "Lindy," 12in (31cm), "Chocolate Drop," 11in (28cm) and "Inky," 13in (33cm), circa 1906 Steiffs.

Another fun September luncheon centerpiece. Besides bears, you need logs, leaves, sticks and, of course, marshmallows!

School Bells Pealing

Out comes the uniform and the backpack — and the school bell is pealing for our young friends in Scotland, also.

Such an appealing face! By artist Sue Quinn, part of a collectors' edition of Dormouse Designs; 15in (38cm), wool and mohair.

SEPTEMBER

A "Haunting" We Will Go

In their 1924 Buddy L truck, driven by a Hallmark witch, is a 1932 oilcloth cat made by Paul in his kindergarten class and *Neddy B* bears made by contemporary artist Suzanne Marks of Newbury Park, California. Spider was also purchased from the Hallmark shop.

Toy trucks are fun to fill with bears and trick or treat goodies.

Greetings from Witch Hazel

— and *Zorastor* (who does magic) on the hall entry table! This time the mirror is framed by grapevines, autumn leaves and bright orange seed pods. Reflected in the mirror you can see 6ft (1.8m) Steiff "Dandy," circa 1970, who has a witch's hat. The bears on the table are by Loretta Botta, 15in (38cm).

OCTOBER

Milkmaid with Cow

— our daughter's third grade class had its first "field trip" recently. They went to a dairy. Such excitement! We were reminded of how many city children have to take such a trip to learn that milk originates some place other than in a cardboard carton. "Country" decorators will be overjoyed with this creation of Lara Zano. The cow is 13in (33cm); milkmaid is 15in (38cm).

Who? Me??

From tales my father told me — an early 1900s trick — turn over the neighbor's outhouse.

Contemporary bear artist Doris King's 13in (33cm) *Huckelbeary* has just the right expression of innocence and guilt.

The "outhouse" was a gift from a Colorado cousin. It is really an extra tissue holder for bathrooms with the very popular "country" motif.

Filled with pumpkins my mother made is a tractor trailer by Structo, circa 1926.

P.S. One year an unknowing victim of Dad's prank offered him $5.00 to return his outhouse to its original state. Dad took it!

Autumn Also Comes —

to the kitchen — with autumn leaves. The blue bear is Lori Gardiner's *Dodger*. On the squash is Flore Emory's *Old Bear*. To the rear right is an Anna Lee bear. In front is Flore Emory's black rag man and Bev Miller's *The Cook*. On the jar of jam is Elaine Gamble's 3in (8cm) *Teddy Baby*.

Carving Pumpkins

Inside the 1930s Gamages' doll house bears by Dickie Harrison and Pat Carriker make jack-o'-lanterns. Notice how neat they are; they put paper down before they began carving. Bears are 1½in (4cm) to 3in (8cm). The pumpkins came from a miniature shop.

Indian and Baby —

by Sarah McClellan made fall just right for the stand in the corner of the hall. The grapevine background also includes orange leaves of plastic. At the base, Anna Lee deer get ready for winter to come. Bear, early 1980s, 18in (46cm).

OCTOBER

Bubble, Bubble, Toil & Trouble

"Bo" and "Dearheart," both circa 1905 Steiff bears 24in (61cm) tall, encountered this witch when they went trick or treating. Dry ice placed in the cauldron with a little water makes a wonderful and realistic window display for All Hallow's Eve!

Haystack Bears —

for those of you who collect only small bears. I made the ghosts costumes of circles of cotton cloth; the masks were made of felt. The devil suit was borrowed from an Anna Lee. The bear with paper mask which we call "Guess Who?" we got at a convention in San Francisco. Smaller bears, 3in (8cm), are contemporary Steiff. Add lanterns but do not light!

In the Pumpkin Patch

"Boo!" Scare you? No, "Don't Shoot!" He is a <u>friendly</u> bear. New design by Linda Spiegel. I smile every time I pass by him! Oh! the colors! My mom made the soft sculpture pumpkins of acrylic, 17in (43cm).

Flight Time!

Ghosts and goblins and a *Bearacula* here and there. Such a funny fellow will not scare anyone! From ABC Productions "Casbear Goes a Haunting" we got a great *Bearacula* by Christine Lamb, 12in (30cm), mohair. His friends are rare Steiff bats.

OCTOBER

Happy Birthday, Dear Teddy — Roosevelt, That Is!

We used a 1910 toy drum with wonderful lithographed Roosevelt bears. In the background is a picture of the famous president himself.

On the drum sits our early American bear, "Sgt. Culver." He is 18in (46cm). He has a canteen marked "GAR" and "We drink from the same canteen," 1861-1865. He came complete with two tickets to the Democratic National Convention in 1888 and 1904, also his own 1914 application to Culver Military Academy in Logansport, Indiana.

Something like this is great if you are in charge of a Salute to Roosevelt at your favorite bear club.

Mr. President

This group includes a bear by contemporary artists Margaret and Gary Nett of Gettysburg, Pennsylvania, 20in (51cm) tall. Doffing his hat is a *T.R.* by Bev Miller of Eugene, Oregon, 13in (33cm) tall. Something new and compatible is a folk art *T.R.* by artist Flore Emory of Escondido, California. Eyeglasses and a top hat are quick Roosevelt transformers for any bear.

There is always a place for Roosevelt bears.

Over the Freeway and Through the Smog

It is still fun to go to Grandmother's house for the Thanksgiving feast! Our hay cart is full of small bears; 6in (15cm), 7in (18cm) and 8in (20cm) by contemporary bear artist Flore Emory. They are taking the pumpkins for pie. You can tell they are very excited to get there!

Pilgrim and Friend

This is great for the "country" enthusiast! This Puritan bear is by contemporary artist Lara Zano of Oregon. She wears an apron filled with a bountiful harvest. Do you sense the friendship between the bear and the bird? I will bet they have corn chowder and pumpkin pie on their feast day. Dress your bear in a bonnet and apron and make her a felt turkey friend. The bear is 16in (41cm) tall and the turkey 11in (28cm).

Falling Leaves and a Tumble Bear

Falling leaves are autumn to me! Here is a sweet combination of a basket filled with all the basic browns and a be-ribboned beige bear.

Contemporary bear artist Jean Woessner of Escondido, California, created *Mitzie*, a 12in (31cm) bear. This bear's pert features (with mink eyelashes) are enhanced by a body with unusual stuffing that allows her to "tumble" into any position you choose to pose her in.

Color Magic

We must not overlook the color magic that autumn winds bring about. This Thanksgiving centerpiece has the purples, mauves and wines that only nature can produce (and man can copy)!

We picked up dried weeds and leaves at a floral supply shop, added some fruit to compliment them and a cornucopia to hold the entire assemblage.

The bear is a masterpiece by contemporary artist Corla Cubillas of Watsonville, California. His perfect color is the result of hand-drying German mohair. His name is *Butterworth* and he is 12in (31cm) tall.

RIGHT:

Good For a Bathroom

A tin pail filled with dried artichoke blossoms and leaves blend with a small bale of hay and little bear by Regina Brock, mohair, 6in (15cm). Accent with ceramic quail on wood bark.

For Whatever
We are About to Receive

— actually, "Bo," our circa 1905, 24in (61cm) Steiff did not fare too well at the turkey shoot, but the Buck Hill bears are truly grateful for the chicken, anyway.

For a centerpiece with whimsy, get your bear a pilgrim's hat and a rubber chicken from your party shop and a blunderbuss from your toy store.

We do hope, however, that your own turkey is a little meatier!

God Bless America!

This country means so much to us and all of the brave men and women who have come to her defense! We MUST remember Veterans Day!

Go to your army surplus store and dress a bear in remembrance of those who, as Lincoln said, "gave their last full measure of devotion....that this nation, under God, shall not perish from the earth."

The bear by Carol Black is 22in (56cm). Musical, it plays "What the World Needs Now."

Up the Stairs

In their usual places we see the "Over the Hill Gang" (all German), over 65 years old and over 30in (76cm) tall. This year they got to open presents! In boxes, beginning at the bottom, we see Steve Schutt's bear with puppet, a circa 1930 Chad Valley bear, Suzanne Marks' *Neddie Bear*, a circa 1930 German Petz bear, a Barbara Sixby *Zukor Bear*, a Cal Toy Original teddy, *Chocolate Parfait* by Joyce O'Sullivan and *Bitte Schoen* by Sherry Baloun.

Unless otherwise noted, all bears are contemporary.

Silver Bells

"Bo" and his gal, "Dearheart," circa 1905 Steiff, 24in (61cm), showcase another family tradition. For over 15 years we have purchased a Wallace Christmas bell for each member of the family. Then we had it engraved with whatever happening was most important that year in each person's life. Obviously, several said, "Welcome to the World."

What do ours say? "Ronald McDonald House, Michigan" and "Disney's 1st Teddy Bear Convention."

A Sleigh Full of Bears

— the Victorian-looking sleigh (in just the right colors) was a gift from a dear lady — Jane Withers! We lined it with old rose foil paper and filled it to running over with Flore Emory's great bears, sized from 6in (15cm) to 7½in (19cm), mohair and acrylic. The bears had fun — and we did, too!

DECEMBER

The Entry Hall — Welcome!

Hurry — scurry and shop without stopping!

Wrapped in scarves and winter caps and equipped with empty shopping bags — off to the mall in their circa 1920s Steiff convertible; the SHOPPERS set the tone of the season!

Back row: "Amanda Rosemary," "Angela" and "Big Rosemary," all contemporary Steiff *Molly* bears, acrylic and cotton, 24in (61cm), 20in (51cm) and 24in (61cm). Front row: "Rosemary Lynn" and "Teri," acrylic, Princess Soft Toy, circa 1970, 17in (43cm) and Lucy Riggs, circa 1988, 17in (43cm).

To the Mall!

Taking a turn on Mary Knestrick's horse this year are "Prudence" and "Pitty Pat." Both are by Avanti, made of polyester plush, 1984. "Prudence" is 30in (76cm); "Pitty Pat" is 10in (25cm).

At the base, peeking out, are a new Steiff *Molly* — acrylic and cotton, 16in (40cm), Bev Port's Time Machine Teddy, *Blue Boy*, 1980, also 16in (40cm) and a Chinese bear.

Mantle Masterpiece

Holly by Carol Black is actually a complete decoration with her garland of lights and bears. She is 15in (38cm), of white mohair. We complimented her pink organdy pinafore with gold garland and pink satin balls. The family portrait above was a 40th anniversary gift from our children.

Perfect for an End Table —

Wendy Brent's bent-knee bear, *Angelique*, 1988, flanked by Volpp grandchildren and Netts' white and cream, 13in (33cm) bears we call "Gary" and "Margaret." All made for each other! *Angelique*, 14in (35cm), was a prototype. She has hand-dyed felt wings and specially made "veined" glass eyes!

DECEMBER

Glass Plus

We inherited some marvelous pieces of glass from Paul's mother. We have learned to take pleasure from things that remind us of her.

Here we added a red-eyed "Yes-No" Schuco fox, circa 1924, 10in (25cm) seated, and a rare Bruin Mfg. Co. bear we call "Wistful," 15in (38cm), 1907. Topped off with pink poinsettias, it takes your breath away!

Cabinet Toppers

Contemporary Steiff, reproduction 1909, 15in (38cm) and 10in (25cm) bears of wool and cotton are some of our favorites. They peek over the top of a cabinet housing another favorite collectible, Lalique crystal pieces.

DECEMBER

Under the Christmas Tree

Decorate <u>under</u> the Christmas tree? Of course! Our Charleen Kinser *Wee Tad*, 1985, 19in (48cm), shares with a new doll, *Punkin,* by Terri De Hetre, vinyl, 21in (58cm). New this year from Kinser are *Miss Lucy* (white) and *McCormick* (brown) mice, 8in (20cm). Such fun!

The koala is by Concepts Plus, Inc., and is from an Olivia Newton-John store. His name is *Blue* which is "Pal" in Aussie. He is 12in (30cm). Peeking around at the left is a *Pooh* from Disney's first teddy bear convention. More about that later. All of these animals are forms of plush.

Cabinet Topper #2

This cabinet is devoted to some of our Nett bears. In the black top hat is the special bear they made for our *Life of Teddy Roosevelt;* it is grand! Mohair with clothing of antique fabric, he is 19in (48cm). No less grand is their Boy Scout! Mohair, 19in (48cm). On top, looking down, we again used the reproduction 1909 Steiff.

DECEMBER

A Focal Point

in any home is the dining room hutch. It is a natural place to display your seasonal dishes, family heirlooms and special glass. This season we set out our Lenox Holiday plates and red cranberry stemware. The small bear, in the tradition of Victorian times, is *Father Christmas* by Lori Gardiner. His robe is made of imported French velvet. He is 16½in (42cm) tall and plays a medley of Christmas carols. At the other end we enjoy Ann Inman's mechanical bears we call "Ann" and "Annette." The big bear moves her head and arms to give the little one a kiss. Mohair, "Ann" is 24in (61cm), little "Annette" 8½in (22cm). The ceramic scene in the middle has Santa telling the forest animals the real meaning of Christmas. It is by our dear friend, Robyn, of Idylwild.

Father Christmas

— a close-up look at Lori Gardiner's Victorian *Father Christmas*. We used him and Lenox Holiday pattern plates to set each other off.

A Doll Among Steiffs

A very <u>special</u> doll! The *Paddy O'Day*, made to commemorate a character in a 1935 movie, was designed by artist Judy Turner (limited edition of 100 only). They are being sold to help fund the Jane Withers' Doll and Teddy Bear Museum — for all the public to enjoy.

The white Steiffs are contemporary, from 30in (76cm) to 2½in (6cm) — wool and cotton. The finishing touch is a *Lucy and Me* Christmas musical Santa-in-Box. The picture is autographed by Jane.

DECEMBER

Chandelier

Working with the tree branches that have been painted white and sprinkled with glitter, we made a branch canopy over our dining room table. Our branches were out 3ft (.91m) in each direction from the chandelier; ours is a 6ft (1.82m) table. Adjust for your own sized table. We also hung glitter stars from the branches. The combined effect was one visitors talked most about.

A Japanese TV crew came and filmed for a show and this was one of their favorites. In keeping with the silver, white, pink and burgandy color scheme, we chose small bears of pink shades. The largest one is *Sandra's Bear* by Amy Jo Boufford, 9in (23cm); the two smaller ones are by Paula Egbert. *Rosie* is 7½in (19cm); *Baby* is 4½in (11cm). All bears are mohair.

Very Special Pillow

— a gift from our daughter. We display it in the living room, held by special bears. Barbara Sixby's *Grandpa MacIntosh* and grandchildren *Pippin* and *Apple Dumpling* won "Best of Show" in Minneapolis a few years ago. The little ones are 20in (51cm). *Grandpa* is 42in (105cm), made of polyester acrylic fabric.

Any Coffee Table

Here we display Barbara McConnell's *Goldilocks and the Three Bears* made of mohair; the bears are 21in (53cm), 20in (51cm) and 8in (20cm). The *Goldilocks*, dressed in pale pink organdy, was imported from Switzerland.

Winter White

describes our living room coffee table this year. Do you recognize the tallest bear on the tray? It is Steiff's beautiful muzzle bear! She has her muzzle in the pink satin lingerie bag. In back is the dear pink-nosed reproduction of 1930 *Teddy Baby* — with wolf — made in limited edition of 1000 for P. Wolff of Gingen. Since we have said the reproduction 1909 is one of our favorites, you know we were pleased with the limited edition for F.A.O. Schwarz this year — only 2000 pieces. All these bears are mohair. *Muzzle Bear* is 19in (48cm), *Teddy Baby* 11½in (29cm) and Schwarz bear 13in (33cm). With the burgundy handmade Battenburg lace collar is *Mrs. Santa Paws*. Made of German plush, she is 20in (51cm). By Wendy Brent.

DECEMBER

Did You See a Doll?

— or maybe two? Our dining table centerpiece featured Carol Black's 14in (36cm) *Baby Got Rocks* (plays "Deck the Halls") with twinkling lights and her own Victorian decorated burgundy basket! And, yes, a doll! In pink organdy (plays "Diamonds Are a Girls Best Friend") — the Diamond Jubilee Issue by Bette Ball to commemorate the 75th anniversary of *Dolly Dingle* (Global Art). The doll is 17in (43cm).

Right for Raikes

We consider the beautifully hand-carved chair by the Bartholomew Co. to be the perfect display piece for a cluster of Raikes bears — and our pride and joy, Bob's hand-carved owl. The owl is 12in (30cm) and dated 1982. *Sebastion* is 21in (53cm) and the little one we renamed "Lady Gray" is 15in (38cm). The last two by Applause, of course.

Favorite People — Favorite Things

Two of our most loved bears, by Hermann, were the brainchildren of Phillips and Edith Rubin. They pioneered "limited" editions and are responsible for the first white bears in the late 1970s.

Edith named these bears *Princess* and *Prince*, 15in (38cm) and 16in (40cm). They are made of short and long curly mohair.

We combined them with a favorite floral piece to bring us pleasant memories of wonderful people!

Phil passed away in 1988 but what a legacy of bears he left us!

Victorian Stocking

Flore Emory's interpretation of the "filled to the toe" Victorian stocking added a lot to our den fireplace this year. It is complete with toys and a 7in (18cm) bear! The bears at the top claim it for their own.

DECEMBER

"Christmas in the Forest"

— was a much wanted gift from my mother-in-law, Bess, over 30 years ago. Notice the ceramic trees have little candies, nuts and cookies? They are actually containers for these items of food. It was Paul's idea to let Santa be telling little bears "the real story of Christmas." We hope you like it, too. The bears are from 1/2in (1cm) to 3in (8cm) and are all by Dickie Harrison except for the one on Santa's knee. It is by Laurie Sasaki.

DECEMBER

Sweetening the Cookie Jar

— a very rare, circa 1920 Steiff "Yes-No" elf with mohair hat. Finding this was an undreamed of Christmas present for us. We always use this gingerbread cookie jar just for this time of year. Let a bear be "in charge" of your cookie jar. The elf is 11in (28cm). Ceramic figures by Robyn of Idyllwild.

At Just the Right Time

— for Christmas! Free puppies! And I would take them all. The pups' mom sits by the cardboard box, longing (with the little boy) for some kind animal lover to stop by and choose a pet. By Julie Zano. The boy is 10in (25cm); puppies are approximately 3½in (9cm).

DECEMBER

"Read to Me, 'Bubby' "

says the naughty sister in the upper bunk who will not go to sleep. "Bub" has parked his airplane and his slippers and is trying oh! so hard to get to sleep so Santa will come. Another visitors' favorite by Botta. The bed is 18in (46cm) long, 16in (41cm) high. The bears are both 12in (31cm).

Yancy Lee

Mickey Mouse was high priority at our house in 1988. Both Mickey and I celebrated our 60th birthday! Another great "portable" decoration we enjoyed was a Mickey Mouse "tree topper" held by Barbara Burbeck's *Yancy Lee*. We added *Lucy and Me* napkins with bear napkin rings for fillers. *Yancy*, 20in (51cm), is German plush, with <u>very</u> special "bunka" Japanese embroidered paw pads and inside ears. Outstanding!

DECEMBER

Ready to Lick the Spoon

— in an abandoned highchair we bought at a toy show, you see Flore Emory's *Mark and his Ted Bear*, all ready for whatever is cooking! *Mark* is 17in (43cm); his bear is 7in (18cm). He has a Christmas sucker — just in case. Also waiting is Barbara Burbeck's *Holly Beary*, 10in (25cm). All bears are acrylic.

Too Many Chefs?

Spoil the feast? Nooo — not when they are North American Bear Co.'s VIBs (Very Important Bears). Sharing the circa 1930s electric stove on our sink top are, in the pale yellow, — and one of the earliest, 1979 *Chef Bernaise* and resplendant in blue with proper attire, *James Beard*. Both bears are 20in (51cm).

Cookie samplers are Anna Lee elves from the late 1970s — also a small assistant Anna Lee chef.

The memory Christmas ornament was from an anniversary stay at the Hotel Del Coronado. Give your bears chefs' hats, aprons and let them cook up some smiles!

DECEMBER

Looking Up — Good Habit!

— you will see squirrels and bears on the range hood. We made it a tree top with artificial leaves. Riding a squirrel is Bev Miller's *Teddy's Attic Santa*, 1984, 9in (23cm). Next is Doris King's *Bunny Slippers Bear*, 13in (33cm) and Linda Spiegel's *Santys Bear*, 10in (23cm). The King bear is mohair; the others are plush.

Hint — Tie all decorations with wire to cabinet knobs. Keep the fire in the fireplace.

The Kitchen Chandelier

From the drug store came the red garland and the gold star garland. They go together beautifully. The bear playing peek-a-boo is the 90th year commemorative bear by Gund, plush, 14in (35cm). He is nicely done and has leather paws.

Smooth O'er the Ice

Ready to try out her new skates, this pert bear by Candy Corvari can lift her legs! Jointing at the knees allows you to position her to run, jump or stand. She also has her own muff to keep her paws warm. Made of mohair, she is 21in (53cm). The snow is cotton. We made this a corner hall table decoration and she did, indeed, "brighten the corner where you are!"

DECEMBER

A Stew of Bears

— on a kitchen sink top. From left: Flore Emory's black, 8in (20cm), with pie rack. Commercial grisly, circa 1980, 6½in (16cm). Flore's big black bear, 17in (43cm), holding country cow bowl by N.S. Gustin Co., USA. Note — dishes are such fun, we sometimes buy only two place settings (for those rare occasions when we eat at home, ha!). *Miss June* by Pauline Weir, 15in (38cm) and *Raggedy Ann* and *Andy* by Barbara Burbeck, 15in (38cm). Finish off with bits of holly and a *Pooh* music box. All bears are plush but "Miss June," which is mohair.

Another Chandelier Treatment

— in the den. We chose as a center a giant Christmas ball with ribbon and greenery. Having fun, swinging in the chandelier are, left: the beautiful new Merrythought bear produced exclusively for Hobby Center this year with the metal hang tag, 17in (43cm); and right: an original circa 1930s Chad Valley whom we call "Sir Laurence" (as in Olivier), 18in (46cm).

DECEMBER

We were chosen to be a part of Disney's 1st Annual Teddy Bear Convention at Epcot Center, Florida.

This etagere is devoted exclusively to bears that were made for the convention. On the top shelf, with the convention banner, is Michaud's *Teddy Snowbird*. On the second shelf, from left, the brown Canterbury bears with cathedral boxes and a black Merrythought with special wishbone. Next is the Hermann bear with tyrolean hat and backpack.

Did We Have Fun?
You know what they say about a picture being worth all those words?

DECEMBER

Rosemary Volpp's *Anything Bea*.

Merry Disney Christmas

On the top shelf of this etagere is the special limited edition *Pooh* Disney had made to commemorate the special event. The hat has embroidery that reads, "Walt Disney World 1st Annual Teddy Bear Convention." A special cloisonne pin was also designed and presented with each bear purchased at the convention. The small *Pooh* was a gift to convention guests. The older yellow bear is our "Lemon Drop Kid" — an Alpha Farnell from the late 1920s (like the one that was the original *Pooh*). The Mickey was a special 50th birthday issue in 1978.

The second shelf is rich with Disney memorabilia, the center of which is the *Teddy Bear and friends®* souvenir issue. Paul had the good fortune to do the cover!

On the third shelf, from the left, the special Steiff with leather paws, another gift *Pooh* and R. John Wright's *Pooh*.

Plumb Tuckered

— under the coffee table. By Flore Emory, 24in (61cm) with great sleepy eyes! He loves his grizly bear, 8in (20cm). He has had so much excitement, he is completely worn out! We wish him — and you, Good Night! Pleasant Dreams!

If you wish to contact any of the Bear Artists mentioned in the book,
here are their addresses and phone numbers at the time of printing:

Adams, Joanne
P.O. Box 55 - Silver Creek
Park City, UT 84060
(801) 649-1368
Ballard Baines Bear Co.
43501 S.E. Cedar Falls Way
North Bend, WA 98045
(206) 888-4441
Baloun, Sherry
7900 N. Milwaukee, Suite 9
Niles, IL 60648
(312) 470-1540
Bartholomews
128 S. Cypress
Orange, CA 92666
(714) 532-4293
Beaver Valley
P.O. Box 678
Etna, CA 96027
(916) 467-5148
Black, Carol
760 Golden Prado Avenue
Diamond Bar, CA 91765
(714) 861-1510
Botta, Loretta
1231 42nd Avenue
San Francisco, CA 94122
(415) 661-8484
Boufford, Amy Jo
237 S. Park
Reed City, MI 49677-1117
Brent, Wendy
135 Elinor Avenue
Mill Valley, CA 94941
(415) 388-3655
Brock, Regina
2621 Brady Lake Road
Ravenna, OH 44266
(216) 296-4866
Burbeck, Barbara
P.O. Box 639
Lucerne Valley, CA 92356
Carriker, Pat
(619) 724-9074
Claustre, Donna
1202 La Brad Lane
Tampa, FL 33613
(813) 961-7158
Cooper, Gail
180 W. Lexington Ave.
Suite 1
El Cajon, CA 92020
Crowe, Nancy
2400 Woodview Drive
Lansing, MI 48911
(517) 372-6788
Cubillas, Corla
112 Montebellow Drive
Watsonville, CA 95076
(408) 722-4718

Davis, Joan
14796 Applewood Lane
Nevada City, CA 95959
(916) 265-6829
De Pee, Heather
De Pee, Suzanne
2208 S. Valley Drive
Visalia, CA 93277
(209) 733-3223
Egbert, Paula
17820 46th Avenue S.
Seattle, WA 98188
(206) 246-2809
Emory, Flore
P.O. Box 1888
Fallbrook, CA 92028
(619) 728-3803
Gamble, Elaine Fujita
9510 232nd SW
Edmonds, WA 98020
(206) 546-0384
Gard, Diane
1005 W. Oak Street
Fort Collins, CO 80521
(303) 484-8191
Gardiner, Lori
2565 S. Mayflower
Arcadia, CA 91006
(818) 447-1775
Grand Papa Jingles
423 Western Avenue
Findlay, OH 45840
(419) 424-1940
Harrison, Dickie
239 Deep Dale Drive
Timonium, MD 21093
(301) 252-1523
Hodges, Donna
P.O. Box 959
La Jolla, CA 92038
(619) 453-2854
Hogan, Beth
5629 N. Bonfair Avenue
Lakewood, CA 90712
(213) 633-3474
Howey, Roy
Howey, Shirley
2064 E. Birchwood
Mesa, AZ 85204
(602) 833-7307
Inman, Ann
11602 Norton Avenue
Chino, CA 91710
(714) 591-4107
Jurdan, Jerry & Morgan
Rt. #1 Box 467
Amboy, WA 98601
(206) 247-5310
King, Barbara
1553 Ridgeway Drive
Glendale, CA 91202
(818) 241-2478

King, Doris
4353 Landolt Avenue
Sacramento, CA 95821
(916) 484-6472
Lamb, Christine
P.O. Box 307
Yucca Valley, CA 92286
(619) 365-6020
Lockwood, Wendy & Kip
2644 Knabe Ct.
Carmichael, CA 95608
(916) 485-6679
Markarian, Eileen
824 W. Maxzim Avenue
Fullerton, CA 92623
(714) 680-4411
Masterson, Karine
435 Montebello Avenue
Ventura, CA 93004
(805) 659-5164
Maul & Paw Bears
P.O. Box 25
Fairview, WV 26570
(304) 449-1293
Rhonda Haught
McClellan, Sara
8622 E. Oak Street
Scottsdale, AZ 85257
(602) 941-8972
McConnell, Barbara
944 W. 9th Avenue
Escondido, CA 92025
(619) 480-1936
Mediate, Flora
190 Malcomb Drive
Pasadena, CA 91105
(818) 796-1220
Michaud, Doris & Terry
505 W. Broad St.
Chesaning, MI 48616
(517) 845-7881
Miller, Bev
87505 Biggs Road
Veneta, OR 97487
(503) 935-7318
Nett, Gary & Margaret
601 Taneytown Road
Gettysburg, PA 17325
(717) 334-2469
Nilan, Kaylee
P.O. Box 678
Etna, CA 96027
(916) 467-5148
O'Sullivan, Joyce
4320 196th S.W., Suite B-233
Lynnwood, WA 98036
(206) 347-1950
Orlando, Cathie
70875 Dillon Rd. #26
Desert Hot Springs, CA 92240
(619) 329-2417

Port, John Paul
922 Highland #202
Bremerton, WA 98310
(206) 373-3243
Pruitts Place
508 Beaumont Dr.
Vista, CA 92083
(619) 758-1150
Quinn, Sue
The Old Drapery
Faith Avenue
Quarriers Village
Renfrewshire
Scotland PA11 3SX
Raikes Bears
P.O. Box 82
Mt. Shasta, CA 96067
(916) 926-4572
Romerhaus Saki Creations
951 S. Alvord Blvd.
Evansville, IN 47714
(812) 473-7277
Rosenbaum, Gloria
259 Beverly Way
Gardnerville, NV 89410
(702) 782-8447
Schutt, Steve
201 1st Avenue N.W.
Clarion, IA 50525
Sixby, Barbara
3965 Duke Court
Livermore, CA 94550
(415) 373-0720
Spiegel, Linda
14776 Moran St.
Westminster, CA 92683
(714) 891-7089
Stafford, Linda
Log Cabin Bears
12116 Redwood Hwy.
Wilderville, OR 97543
(503) 474-0639
Warlow, Gerry
30 John St.
Rosewood 4340,
Queensland, Australia
(07) 564-1479
Woessner, Joan
P.O. Box 27920
Escondido, CA 92027
(619) 746-5132
Wright, Beverly
890 Patrol Road
Woodside, CA 90462
(415) 851-7017
Zano, Julie
1618 Chemawa NE
Salem, OR 97303
(503) 393-3793
Zano, Lara
1618 Chemawa NE
Salem, OR 97303
(503) 393-3793